RVC Liturgical Series

Nancy Benvenga, Series Editor

No. 3

The Liturgy of the Hours: Your Guide to Praying at Home and in Your Parish Community

Resurrection Press
Mineola, New York

Nihil obstat: Rev. Msgr. John A. Alesandro, S.T.L., J.C.D.
Censor librorum
January 25th, 1990

Imprimatur: Most Reverend John R. McGann, D.D.
Bishop of Rockville Centre
January 31st, 1990

Original articles © Office of Catechesis and Worship, Diocese of Rockville Centre

Compilation © 1990 by Resurrection Press

Illustrations and front cover design: William Hanson

Music excerpt © Christoph Tietze, Music Director, St. Agnes Cathedral, Rockville Centre

First published in 1990 by: Resurrection Press
P.O. Box 248
Williston Park, NY 11596

ISBN 0-9623410-7-X

All rights reserved. No part of this book may be reproduced or transmitted in any form or by any means, electronic or mechanical, including photocopying, recording or by any information storage and retrieval system without permission in writing from the publisher.

Printed in the United States of America by Faith Printing.

Contents

THE LITURGY OF THE HOURS: A WAY TO "PRAY ALWAYS."
   Christopher Heller 1

PRAYER OF PRAISE. *John Gurrieri* 3

THE PSALMS: PRAYERS OF LIFE. *Nancy Benvenga* 17

IMPLEMENTING THE LITURGY OF THE HOURS
   IN THE PARISH. *Ronald Hayde* 23

MUSICAL RESOURCES 31

RESOURCES AND PUBLISHERS 34

About the Authors

Dr. Nancy Benvenga is a liturgical minister at St. Agnes Cathedral, Rockville Centre, N.Y.

Rev. John Gurrieri is former Director of the Bishops' Committee on the Liturgy Secretariat.

Rev. William Hanson (artist) is Associate Pastor at St. Martin of Tours, Amityville, N.Y.

Rev. Ronald Hayde is Associate Pastor at St. Christopher, Baldwin, N.Y., and Assistant Director for Music/Liturgy for the Diocese of Rockville Centre, N.Y.

Rev. Christopher Heller is Diocesan Liturgy Coordinator for the Diocese of Rockville Centre, N.Y.

List of Abbreviations

LG   Dogmatic Constitution on the Church *(Lumen Gentium)*, 1964
LOH General Instruction of the Liturgy of the Hours, 1971

The Liturgy of the Hours: A Way to "Pray Always"

I am a convert to the Liturgy of the Hours. It was not always a part of my personal or communal prayer life, nor did I readily accept it when people offered the Hours as a viable prayer form. I had all the objections: its structure and content were too rigid, the psalms were unfamiliar and mysterious, my elders treated it as a penance and raced to finish it, and the chapel was too cold. One of the initiated then reminded me of an axiom from our youth: we crawl before we walk. As dancers and choreographers tell us, we need to learn and respect the steps before we will understand the freedom and flexibility they contain. To put it another way, wisdom becomes a reality only when we become one with the inner movement. Like the slice of cantaloupe my parents insisted I taste over my objections, and which I later came to enjoy, so it was that my praying the Hours became an experience of seeing and knowing the Lord's goodness.

Our tradition reminds us of four varieties in prayer: petition, adoration, contrition and thanksgiving. Whether prompted by life's tempestuous seas or in response to the Lord's gospel mandate to ask and seek, we have become virtual experts in the art of petition. The Liturgy of the Hours inverts the order, and proposes that we become first and always a people who offer God thanksgiving and praise. Morning Prayer is "get up and go" prayer. It acknowledges God as source of life and offers thanks for the gift of early light and deliverance from night's darkness. Evening Prayer constitutes a summation of the day's journey. At sunset or dusk we gather to render praise for the blessings received and ask for protection through the night to come. As in a balanced diet, priorities are established while other elements complement and supplement the nucleus. Choosing appropriate music and lighting enhances and establishes a prayerful environment. Including symbols such as the paschal candle and incense localizes our primeval and multivalent hunger for the Transcendent One.

The Liturgy of the Hours is authentic liturgy, the work of God's people united in prayer with Christ Jesus. This becomes extremely clear when we recall the ways in which the Lord is present: in the assembly gathered for worship, in the ministers, and in the Word proclaimed. While we treasure and value the Eucharist as an incomparable peak experience, it should not exhaust our spiritual nourishment. Through sound and silence, the Hours can provide harmony and balance for pilgrims who seek the face of God in their daily journeys.

If we Christians are better to appreciate that our prayer heritage extends longer than our memories or that of our grandparents, we need a fundamental respect for the ways in which the Jewish people, including Jesus, engaged in prayer. The psalms have often been called the prayer book of the Church, for we have adopted them as prayer-songs which express our own sentiments and desires. Which of us has not at one time or another cried out to God, "Be with me, Lord, when I am in trouble" or "My soul is longing for your peace, O God, my God"?

To conclude, the Liturgy of the Hours is the Church's response to Christ's command to pray always. Through the night and day, we acknowledge our dependence on the Lord who crushes the darkness by his light. Adapting this prayer form for parish use is a worthy goal. A parish in which I resided successfully introduced Sunday evening Vespers to an appreciative praying community for Lent and Advent. No longer confined to the dwellers of monastery, convent or rectory, the Liturgy of the Hours has become a viable option for local communities. It is well worth our time and energy to share this discoverable gift with one another.

Prayer of Praise

The Lord Jesus taught his disciples "the necessity of praying always and not losing heart" (Lk 18:1). Prayer is among the first duties of the Church and "the Church has faithfully heeded this exhortation, for it never ceases to pray and urges us to do so" (LOH, #10). Nor did Jesus leave the Church to flounder in succeeding ages to discover ways and means to pray, for the Lord taught the Church *how* to pray, and *when* to pray, and even to define herself in terms of prayer.

Baptized Christians become the Church and express themselves as Church through prayer and worship. When they engage themselves in the public work (liturgy) of praise, especially in the Sunday eucharistic assembly, they are most evident as "Church." Moreover, the public and communal prayer of the people of God is not only the duty of the Church, it is also the "school of life" in which Christians learn to hear and discern the voice of the hidden God, and learn with what voice to respond to his word. All prayer is dialogue.

The Nature of Liturgical Prayer

The contemporary rediscovery of praying daily through the Liturgy of the Hours is another attempt on the Church's part to rediscover the roots of Christian prayer, particularly Christian liturgical prayer. The ritual reform of the past decades has not been an effort to recodify or create new "rubrics," or even to invent rites to beguile, mystify and annoy us. Rather, liturgical reform is concerned with the revival of liturgical prayer. What is liturgical prayer? Why all the fuss? Aren't Christians praying anyway?

All prayer, particularly liturgical prayer, is dialogue. If revelation is God speaking "in fragmentary and varied ways to our fathers through the prophets" and finally to us through his Son (Heb 1:1-2), the living Word made flesh (Jn 1:14), the Word who speaks to us and who is the very speech of God (Jn 1:3-4), then the proper response to this God who unfolds his being to us must be accomplished in the only way possible to us: hearers of the word speak in the language of the Word, and in the voice of the Word. In brief, a dialogue is arranged whereby men and women respond to the hidden God in the only way he has revealed himself: through his Son, the Word.

Liturgical prayer is dialogue precisely because God speaks and we must respond. Naturally enough there is no symmetry in this dialogue (our speech and God's speech are generically different). Yet there is a semantic and symbolic structure in which the dialogue is possible, and does in fact occur. And the first fact of that structure of liturgical prayer is the liturgical *assembly* itself.

Prayer and the Mystery of Assembly

For St. Paul the Christian "mystery" is the eternal plan of salvation hidden in God from the beginning, now revealed and accomplished in Jesus Christ. It is the communication of the invisible through the visible humanity of Christ and, since his return to the Father, in the sacraments, the visible signs of salvation in the Church. What was seen in Christ, Leo the Great tells us, is manifested now in the "mysteries," the sacraments, of the Church. It is in the same sense that Vatican II spoke of the Church, particularly the assembly of the local church, as a sacrament, "a sign and instrument . . . of communion with God and unity among all" (LG, #1).

The work of this assembly, in order for it to be the sign of communion and unity, is prayer. The assembly gathers to hear God's word and to respond to that word. Thus the second fact of liturgical prayer is that it is *communal:* the dialogue between

God and the Christian is really the dialogue of God and the Christian assembly, for the assembly is where the Church becomes the sign of the people of the Covenant. Christ came to proclaim and accomplish the eschatological gathering announced by the prophets. The liturgical assembly is the sign of that eschatological gathering of the heavenly banquet. To be a Christian is to be communal, and to engage in Christian prayer is first to pray "where two or more are gathered" (Mt 18:20).

Yet liturgical prayer is not simply left up to the invention of Christians in every age (although Christians of every age keep discovering forms of prayer). It is essentially prayer that is *mediated by Christ* and *revealed by Christ*. The Lord Jesus left us actions to follow and build upon, and the history of liturgical prayer is the story of the development of words and forms, symbols and rites which have expanded the core of Christ's action-revelation, the sacramental legacy of Christ and the Church.

If liturgical prayer is mediated by the Word it is nevertheless a human activity in which Christians in assembly engage. Thus its structure consists in the balance of biblically rooted (that is, handed down by the Word) types or genres of prayer. Historically, these types are glorification *(doxologia)*, thanksgiving *(eucharistia)*, penance *(exomologesis)* and petition. The dialogue between God and the Christian assembly is rooted in and expressed through these genres of prayer. Moreover, they are types appropriate to the human condition: creatureliness.

For though we must give thanks to our Creator and Savior, though we need to do penance, seek forgiveness and petition the Lord for those things necessary to our sustenance, we must nevertheless constantly praise, "give glory," to the Father, even in times of distress and anxiety. Doxology is the mark of prayer which ultimately signals Christian prayer (as it does Jewish prayer).

While liturgical prayer is structure in all four types of prayer, the only proper response of the Church to God is to glorify the Lord, and this through the "glory of the Father," Jesus Christ. Liturgical prayer therefore is always *christological:* it is Christ in whose death and resurrection we are initiated; it is Christ who offers himself in the Eucharist, and we who share in that offering are glorified with him and "filled with his Holy Spirit." The christological nature of liturgical prayer means also that the assembly of the faithful at prayer is associated with, or more accurately is the mirror image of, the worship that Christ himself renders to his Father through his Body the Church accomplished in prayers, rites and signs that make accessible to the mind and senses what essentially must remain hidden and inaccessible: the mystery of God.

Liturgical prayer, mediated by Christ ("through him, with him, in him"), is accomplished in the power of the Holy Spirit; thus, liturgical prayer is *pneumatological.* We are able to pray, St. Basil says, because "our spirits, enlightened by the Holy Spirit, fix their sights on the Son, and in him [as in an image] contemplate the Father." The Spirit is the power behind Christian prayer enabling us to say, "Abba, Father" (Rom 8:15).

Finally, liturgical prayer is *eschatological.* At the heart of the Church's prayer is the desire for the return of Christ *(marana tha):* for the dialogue between the Christian and God, his heavenly Father, raises the Christian's consciousness as to the vulnerability of his situation in life. This in turn demonstrates the provisional quality of all human accomplishments, and gives hope "until he comes in glory," in spite of suffering and setback.

Liturgical Prayer Is Paschal

If liturgical prayer is eschatological, it is also rooted in time: each moment of life, and of prayer, is transparent to the paschal mystery. This is not made holy, so much as it is revealed as the age of the coming of the fullest glory of God's revelation. Time itself is eschatologically and future-oriented. The core of this orientation is the paschal event, the mystery of Christ's dying and rising and coming again. The Christian Sunday as the "Eighth Day" is the highest example of liturgical eschatology, for the very nature of the week as the progression of seven days is shattered by the resurrection of the Lord on the first day of creation. The Lord's Day makes the counting of days nearly impossible, for Sunday is an apocalyptic day, a vision of the celestial liturgy mirrored on earth in the eucharistic assembly — a vision of the glory of God in the Risen Son.

The liturgical year, on the other hand, is no more than an expansion of what we do on Sunday: the annual feast of Easter, the seasons which prepare and extend the celebration are present in concentrated form in the Sunday Eucharist. And just as the liturgical year expands on both sides of Easter, so too the Christian week of days develops from the Sunday assembly. Each day is given meaning because of its relationship to Sunday, the day of the resurrection; for example, Friday = day of crucifixion, and so forth. So too, in the tradition of the Church each hour of each day is related to the paschal sequence of events, and to the Sunday Eucharist. This is especially true in the Liturgy of the Hours which "extends to the different hours of the day the praise and prayer, the memorial of the mysteries of salvation and the foretaste of heavenly glory, which are offered to us in the eucharistic mystery, 'the center and culmination of the entire life of the Christian community' " (LOH, #12).

Consecration of Time

The succession of Christian festivals occurs throughout the year, sanctifying time, relating earthly time to the once-for-all event of Christ's passover. Each feast takes us out of successive time and places us within a universe in which the days and the hours are not counted. The Liturgy of the Hours operates in much the same way: at each hour in which the Christian assembly gathers to celebrate the paschal mystery (e.g., Morning Prayer, Evening Prayer, etc.), the community mirrors the unceasing heavenly liturgy.

The revised Office attempts to clarify the relationship of human life and consecrated time:

> Since the Liturgy of the Hours is supposed to sanctify the day with all of its activities, the traditional sequence of the Hours has been restored so that, as far as possible, the proper Hour can be celebrated at the proper time of day. (LOH, #11)

The Liturgy of the Hours, then, is concerned with the restoration of true canonical time so that each hour may be celebrated with spiritual advantage. While the modern conditions in which daily life has to be lived are to be taken into account, nevertheless the strong tradition of praying at certain hours of the day, particularly in the morning and evening, are to be retained. And time is sanctified by the celebration of the Office because it is the exercise of Christ's priestly praise of glory.

Priestly Praise of Glory

In the Liturgy of the Hours Christ's priestly ministry is exercised because he is present in his paschal mystery when the

Church gathers in assembly to praise the Father. Thus the Church exercises the priestly office of Christ the Head, never ceasing to offer God a sacrifice of praise — a sacrifice offered by the lips of men and women when they acknowledge God's name. The very essence of liturgical prayer as doxology is evident in the Liturgy of the Hours because the Church joins in singing a canticle of praise sung throughout all ages in the halls of heaven; it is the foretaste of the heavenly praise sung unceasingly before the throne of God and the Lamb, as described by John in the Apocalypse (LOH, #16).

The *General Instruction of the Liturgy of the Hours* over and over again asserts that the Office is the mirror of the heavenly liturgy because it is so perfectly a prayer of praise before it is anything else, praise in the eschatological dimension:

> The prophets saw this heavenly liturgy as a victory of day over night, a victory of light over darkness: "No longer shall the sun give you daylight, nor the brightness of the moon shine upon you; the Lord shall be your light for ever; your God shall be your splendor" (Is 60:19; cf. Rev 21:23, 25). "The day will be one continuous day; only the Lord knows when it will come. There will be no distinction between day and night; in evening it will be light" (Zech 14:7). . . . The renovation of the world has been irrevocably determined, and it is, in a real way, already anticipated in this age. Our faith teaches us the meaning of our earthly life so that we may await with every creature the revelation of the children of God. In celebrating the Liturgy of the Hours we proclaim this faith, we express and nourish this hope, and we share the anticipated joy of praising God in that eternal day which will have no end. (#16)

Time is consecrated through the priestly office of the Church offering incessant praise to God. There is no day or night, neither beginning nor end: praise is unceasing because we are caught up in the eternal praise of the heavenly court. In the Liturgy of the Hours we are already living in the eschatological age. For this reason it is a "divine office." It is an "office" in the sense of the Latin word *officium,* a charge, an occupation, that is, a public and ritual activity of the community. And it is "divine" in this sense, that it consists entirely in the praise of God. The "divine office" that is the Liturgy of the Hours is the fulfillment of the essential task of the Church: incessant praise of God by the priestly people of God.

Structure of the Hours

In community celebration and in individual recitation, this liturgy remains essentially the same: a dialogue between God and man. It is, nevertheless, a celebration which shows most clearly the ecclesial nature of the Liturgy of the Hours, since it allows and encourages everyone to participate in their own proper way with acclamations, responses, alternating psalmody, and other elements. It also permits different forms of expression. Therefore, whenever it is possible to celebrate the Liturgy in common with the active participation of the people, this form is preferable to individual and quasi-individual recitation. . . . In this way the apostle Paul's exhortation will be fulfilled: "Let the word of Christ, with all its richness, dwell within you. In wisdom made perfect, instruct and admonish one another. Sing thankfully to God from the heart in psalms, hymns, and inspired songs" (Col 3:16; cf. Eph 5:19-20). (LOH, #33)

Basic to the structure of the Liturgy of the Hours (as a whole and to each of the individual hours) are the concepts of *dialogue* and *participation:* the dialogue between God and his people celebrated in common by the local assembly clearly demonstrates the ecclesial nature of the Divine Office. Each hour is organized as a dialogue: God speaking through psalms and readings, the Church responding through hymns, canticles and psalms. The dialogue becomes intense when the assembly celebrates it through active participation.

Morning and Evening Prayer

"In keeping with the ancient tradition of the universal Church, Morning and Evening Prayer form a double hinge of the daily Office and are therefore to be considered the principal Hours and celebrated as such" (LOH, #37). Both Morning and Evening Prayer are structured in the same way, with the same basic elements: opening hymn, psalmody, Scripture reading, canticle, prayers. "Morning Prayer is intended and arranged for the sanctification of the morning. . . . This Hour, celebrated as it is as the light of a new day is dawning, also recalls the resurrection of the Lord Jesus, the true light enlightening all" (LOH, #38). Evening Prayer, celebrated in the evening as the day draws to a close, "in order that we may give thanks for what has been given us . . . during the day," brings to mind the mystery of redemption. For Evening Prayer is like the evening sacrifice of incense, and especially like the sacrifice "which was offered in the evening by the Lord and Savior at supper with the apostles when he instituted the most holy mysteries of the Church" (LOH, #39). Thus Morning and Evening Prayer are the most important Hours of the Office, and should be celebrated publicly and communally by the Church, in parishes and in groups of the faithful (LOH, #40).

Office of Readings

Next in importance in the Liturgy of the Hours is the Office of Readings, which "seeks to provide God's people, and in particular those consecrated to God in a special way, with an ampler selection of prayers from Sacred Scripture for meditation, together with the finest extracts from spiritual writers" (LOH, #55). Usually the Office of Readings may be celebrated at any time of day since it does not have the character of a particular time or hour of the day.

Daytime and Night Prayer

From the earliest years Christians have paused at various times in the course of the day's work and prayed privately for a few moments. This they do in imitation of the apostolic Church. Over the centuries this tradition has been linked in different ways to liturgical prayer. (LOH, #74)

As we have seen, the "Little Hours" (Terce, Sext, None) have traditionally been associated with moments in the mystery of the Lord's Passion and death, and the first preaching of the Gospel. Each of these daytime hours has the same structure. Those who are commissioned with the duty of celebrating the Office in choir are obliged to pray these hours. Only one hour need be said by others "so that the tradition of prayer in the course of the day's work may be maintained" (LOH, #77).

"Night Prayer is the last prayer of the day, said before retiring at night, even after midnight" (LOH, #84).

Night Prayer begins in the usual way with the introductory

verse which may be followed by an examination of conscience either in silence, or using one of the penitential acts provided (LOH, #86). A suitable hymn follows for each night. Psalms which evoke confidence in God are chosen for the weekdays, while Psalms 4, 133 and 90 are provided for Saturday and Sunday nights. After the psalmody, there is a brief reading followed by the traditional *in manus tuas* responsory. There follows the canticle *Nunc dimittis* with its antiphon, "Protect us, Lord." The concluding prayer is said followed by the final blessing. Then, as in the former Office, one of the antiphons of the Blessed Virgin is sung or said.

Praying the Psalms

The psalms are the prayers of the People of the Covenant, and therefore of the Church, and as such they are a veritable mine of prayer. They have universal bearing, for in them one perceives the existential and salvific situation of a people oppressed, a people crying out to God, a people being saved, a people at worship, a people in joyful procession. Even though many psalms are written in the first person "I," the experience is more than personal. In the psalms we don't pray for others, not even in the name of others, but rather it is the *people,* God's Covenant People, God's Church, that is praying. And even the individual praying a psalm in solitary retreat is in communion with the People of the Psalms.

In this sense it is easy to see the christological significance of the psalms: Christ is the hope of the Covenant and the fulfillment of the Covenant. It is also Christ who prays the psalms; the psalms are also about Jesus Christ. Nevertheless, to say that the psalms are Christian prayer is not to experience them as such. The *General Instruction* recognizes the problem, and encourages, as did the *Constitution on the Liturgy,* not just education about the Scriptures and the psalms, but initiation into their deeper, mystagogical significance. At the same time, an appreciation of their literal meaning is important because it is there we find the emotions of the psalmist most poignant and most like our own. Each psalm was composed in historical context, but its universality lies in the experience of the individual psalmist. This literal meaning is necessary not only for our proper understanding of the psalms but also for their proper singing and celebration.

And the psalms are song. They are the poetry of the temple, the poetry of the suffering servant of God, the poetry of human isolation, the poetry of human joy. They are best experienced when they are musically celebrated. Common celebrations of the Liturgy of the Hours ought, by the very nature and structure of the Divine Office, to be sung celebrations — especially the psalmody.

"In the Latin tradition there are three valuable aids to understanding the psalms and making them truly Christian prayer: the headings, the psalm prayers, and especially the antiphons" (LOH, #110).

Psalm headings are provided for each psalm in the Psalter of the Divine Office "to indicate its meaning and its importance in Christian life." They are given as aids for the person or community praying. "A phrase from the New Testament or from the fathers is also given to add to the psalms the dimension of Christ's new revelation and to help make them a Christian prayer" (LOH, #111).

The **psalm prayer** helps those "who say the psalms to see them in a Christian light. It is an old tradition" now restored "that after the psalm and a silent pause, a short, collect prayer is said summing up the thoughts and feelings of the people" (LOH, #112).

Finally, each psalm has its own **antiphon** "to be said whether the liturgy is sung by a congregation or recited by an individual." The antiphon helps illustrate the literary character of the psalm. But they also "turn the psalm into a personal prayer and they highlight a certain significant phrase which might otherwise be missed." Likewise they "give special color to a psalm in accord with different occasions; though they avoid arbitrary accommodations of meaning, they do help us to see in the psalm the typology and theme of the current feast." Thus the singing or recitation of the psalms becomes "more attractive and varied" (LOH, #113).

Scripture Readings

"Following ancient tradition, Sacred Scripture is read publicly in the Liturgy, not only in the celebration of the Eucharist, but also in the Liturgy of the Hours" (LOH, #140).

The *liturgical* reading of the Scriptures is important to Christians "because it is based on the decision of the Church itself and not upon an individual's own inclination" (LOH, #140). The proclamation of the word of God unfolds the mystery of Christ over the course of the year, and is accompanied by prayer so that we may "hear the reading more fruitfully and pray — especially in the psalms — with greater understanding and deeper devotion" (LOH, #140).

The arrangement of the readings in the Liturgy of the Hours takes two principles into account: "the special seasons of the year during which certain books are traditionally read, and the sequence of readings at Mass" to which the readings in the Office are linked. "In this way the history of salvation can be viewed as a whole" (LOH, #143).

Intercessions and Prayers

"The Liturgy of the Hours is a celebration in praise of God. Jewish and Christian tradition does not separate prayer of petition from praise of God; often enough, praise turns somehow to petition" (LOH, #179).

While the essential nature of the Liturgy of the Hours may be said to be doxology and praise, the praise of God leads naturally to feeling at ease in the presence of the mighty God. Praise instills devotion and awe in the one who glorifies, and devotion leads to a certain facility in conversation with the Holy God who does not even need our praise:

> You have no need of our praise, yet our desire to thank you is itself your gift. Our prayer of thanksgiving adds nothing to your greatness, but makes us grow in grace through Jesus Christ our Lord. (Preface 20)

Moreover, to pray and intercede for others *is* the praise of God: "There should be prayers offered for everyone.... To do this is right, and will please God our Savior: he wants everyone to be saved and reach full knowledge of the truth" (1 Tim 2:1-4). The intercessions and prayers of the Liturgy of the Hours express this reality: to petition the Lord is to praise him. So we pray *for* the whole Church, for the Liturgy of the Hours is the prayer *of* the whole Church. General intentions should always have first place, as in the *General Instruction* at Mass. Prayer is made for those who hold civil authority, for those who suffer poverty, disease, sorrow or oppression. Finally, particular needs of the community are commended to God.

In the new liturgical scheme, the Lord's Prayer is now solemnly recited or sung three times a day: at Lauds, at Mass and at Vespers. The Lord's Prayer follows the intercessions and prayers, and is in turn followed by the concluding Prayer of the Day at Lauds and Vespers. This prayer completes the whole Hour.

Sacred Silence

The restoration of sacred silence to liturgical celebrations is an important element that is not always appreciated, though it is often extolled. The purpose of silence, at Mass and in the Liturgy of the Hours, is to allow the voice of the Holy Spirit to be heard more fully in our hearts, "and to unite our personal prayer more closely with the word of God and the public voice of the Church" (LOH, #202).

Silence can be introduced into the Office in several ways: after the psalm; after the reading; before or after the responsory. However, "care must be taken to avoid the kind of silence that would disturb the structure of the Office, or embarrass and weary those taking part" (LOH, #202). Silence should be a part even of the individual recitation of the Office.

Music

> The sung celebration of the Divine Office is the form which best accords with the nature of this prayer. It is a sign of fuller solemnity and expresses a more profound union of hearts in celebrating the praises of God. For these reasons, this sung form is strongly recommended to those who celebrate the Office in choir or in common. (LOH, #268)

What the Second Vatican Council said about singing at the Eucharist applies to the Liturgy of the Hours, as it does to every other liturgical action. While the Office has been arranged so that it can be recited, "singing in the Liturgy of the Hours is not something purely ornamental or extrinsic to prayer. It springs from the depths of a person who prays and praises God and reveals fully and perfectly the communal character of Christian worship" (LOH, #270). Singing the Office is no more a task for ideal monastic communities than singing the Mass. It is quite possible for parishes to sing Morning and/or Evening Prayer.

As with singing at the Eucharist, care, planning and competent musical leadership are required. The simplest of Gregorian or other forms of chant are quite accessible to modern congregations, and in the past years most congregations have built a reputable repertory of hymns.

Pastoral Challenge

The Liturgy of the Hours offers the Church a pastoral challenge on two fronts: personal and ecclesial. The question of liturgical prayer is still a salient one for us, and we are still in the process of forming attitudes in celebrants and congregations that enable us to understand what principles underlie good liturgical prayer. Perhaps the most important thing that has yet to happen is the interiorization of worship. The Divine Office challenges us to do just that — to sanctify and express the sanctity of the day we live hour by hour. A new attitude is needed personally by those canonically obliged to the Office and those who are not. A new vision is necessary in pastors or parishes which will offer opportunities for the celebration of the Hours in a communal setting. The Liturgy of the Hours must be seen as a fitting way to praise God for individuals, small groups and parish communities. In his Apostolic Constitution *Laudis Canticum* (Nov. 1, 1970) promulgating the Divine Office, Pope Paul offered a magnificent vision for the Church at praise:

> Let divine praise ring out, therefore, more splendidly and beautifully in the Church of our times. Let it unite with the praise of the saints and the angels resounding in the heavenly mansions and, growing in perfection, let it approach more and more, in the days of this earthly exile, that full praise that is given forever "to him who sits upon the throne and to the Lamb" (Rev 5:13).

The Psalms: Prayers of Life

The psalms form the backbone of the Liturgy of the Hours. Within the course of a four-week cycle all 150 psalms are prayed, with the exception of three reserved for Advent, Christmas, Lent and Eastertide, and three that are omitted from the four-week psalter because of their "imprecatory character" (LOH, #131).

Thus if we are to feel at home with praying the Liturgy of the Hours we must feel at home with the psalms. We must familiarize ourselves with their rhythms, their language and modes of expression. Above all we must open ourselves to experience the psalms as *our prayer:* they belong to us as individuals and as members of Christ's Body, the Church. Jesus prayed these beautiful prayers while he lived on earth, and he continues to pray them with us, his people, whenever we gather to pray in his name. The psalms "offer . . . a foretaste of the fullness of time revealed in Christ our Lord and from which the prayer of the Church receives its strength" (LOH, #101).

As scriptural prayer the psalms are the inspired word of God and, therefore, like God himself they transcend time. They speak to and for all people at all times. They describe every conceivable situation, express the entire range of human emotions — from peace in God's love for us to seething rage at an unjust fate — with no holds barred. In short, the psalms encapsulate the human condition and present it with all its joys, pain, hopes and ecstasy to God. Whether we want to "come before him, singing for joy" (Ps 100) or to "pour out our hearts before him" (Ps 62), the psalms give us the words.

Prayer Themes in the Psalms

This is by no means a rigid classification! Many psalms overlap into more than one theme; for example, many nuggets of "wisdom" can be found in "praise" psalms. Rather, this is merely a taste of the riches contained in the psalms. As you grow in love of and familiarity with the psalms you will undoubtedly discover others which you could make a note of under the appropriate theme; or you may even wish to add new themes of your own.

PRAISE AND WORSHIP. Most of the psalms with a straightforward praise theme joyfully acknowledge God's power over and care for creation (e.g., Ps 104). Pray them if you are moved to acclaim the Lord as Savior (Ps 95), as shepherd (Ps 100) or as a mighty yet compassionate God (Ps 113); or when you want to meditate upon God's faithfulness to his people (Ps 105).

Some of the praise psalms can nourish our meditation on the marvels of God's creation and our place in it (Ps 8), while others (e.g., Ps 47) specifically praise God as a great and loving King.

THANKSGIVING. In the psalms the rendering of thanks is not an "I-God" transaction but an "I-community" one. For God's goodness to me I praise him before all the people. "In the Lord my soul shall boast; the humble will hear and be glad" (Ps 34). Why will the humble be glad? Because what God has done for me he can do for them, if they but call upon his name. Ps 116 is a thanksgiving psalm *par excellence.*

Psalms which acclaim GOD'S GOODNESS, COMPASSION AND LOVE are thanksgiving psalms that particularly emphasize God's love for us as individuals. A most beautiful example is Ps 103. When we are moved to celebrate God's love and care for the individual soul we can also pray Ps 145 ("The Lord is near to all who call him").

CONFIDENCE IN GOD. With these psalms we can meditate on God's loving care, finding in it a source of comfort or of strength. What better example could there be than Ps 23, the "Good Shepherd" psalm? Pss 16 and 131 are the ultimate declarations of confidence in God and the peace it brings.

LONGING FOR GOD. When we are seized by a yearning for the infinitude of God, certain psalms can be a valuable aid to prayer. The longing voiced in Ps 43 springs from the exile's yearning for his homeland, but it can be an expression of the deep yearning for and openness to God experienced by any of us.

Pss 42 and 63 use thirst imagery to describe the soul's longing for God. As the body cannot survive without water, so too does the soul depend on God to nourish its life.

PETITIONS FOR PROTECTION AND STRENGTH. These psalms call upon God's strength-giving protection as a constant, abiding presence in our lives. With Ps 25 we appeal to the Lord to reveal his ways to us and to protect us against our enemies, and in Ps 61 we ask him, "Hide me in the shelter of your wings." The imagery of a parent bird protecting its young occurs frequently in the psalms as well as in other parts of the Bible.

GENERAL DISTRESS. In these psalms we begin by recalling God's help in the past. Then we declare our confidence that he will come to our aid again — and so complete is this confidence that we promise to praise and thank God for hearing our prayer, and indeed, to thank him publicly. We thereby become a living testimony to God's love.

Should I wish to pour out my distress to the Lord in the true psalm tradition I can do no better than to pray Ps 22, "My God, my God, why have you forsaken me?" From its initial searing pain it progresses through petition for God's help to a promise to praise him when he has heard my prayer. This note of optimism in the distress psalms can truly assist us in focusing and expressing our faith and hope in a God who cares for us. Ps 69, too, promises that "the poor when they see [God's help] will be glad."

APPEAL FOR JUSTICE, PROTECTION AGAINST FOES. Whether I have been the object of gossip, the victim of crime or rejected by a loved one, these psalms offer a wealth of help for pouring out my feelings before God. For example, I can identify with the psalmist who depicts himself as unfairly accused by an enemy (Ps 35), or deplore the seemingly unjust situation by which the wicked thrive while the good suffer (Ps 58).

Many of these psalms vent extreme anger and call upon God to strike the enemy down. And yet even our anger and frustration are tempered by hope in God's loving care, for we promise to praise and thank God for coming to our aid.

GENERAL SORROW. As the People of God we believe that the tragedy which affects our brothers and sisters affects us as well, and therefore we can turn to these eloquent psalms (e.g.,

Pss 79, 80) for support after any major disaster, whether it be an earthquake, a drought or the bombing of an airplane.

The REPENTANCE psalms are among the most valuable, because in praying them we can come to discern the true nature of repentance and of the relationship between God and ourselves as penitents. They show us a God who teaches us his ways, who lets his Spirit guide us, who is the source of the grace of wisdom (Ps 51). Ps 32 conveys a profound psychological truth: that only in acknowledging our shortcomings and weaknesses before God can we open ourselves to his healing.

The WISDOM psalms might also be called the "ways of living" psalms. By describing what a good person is like and contrasting him or her with the evil or foolish person, they provide us with food for thought on how to seek out God's paths. Ps 1 contrasts the person "whose delight is in the law of the Lord" with the wicked whose ways "lead to doom."

If we pray carefully and openly, God will reveal to us nuggets of wisdom in many different kinds of psalms: nuggets which nourish, nuggets which challenge, which make us think. In Ps 80 we pray, "You brought a vine out of Egypt; to plant it you drove out the nations." What did God drive out in order to plant *my* vine? What does he wish to drive out from within myself, what weakness or insecurities? How else does he clear the ground — clear the way, clear my life — in order to plant and let flourish the vine of my relationship with him?

Ps 108 asks, "But who will lead me to conquer the fortress? Who will bring me face to face with Edom?" The problems and pains we encounter are to be confronted, not side-stepped or "put up with." God expects this as a part of our path to holiness, and he is always there with his saving grace, to "lead us to conquer the fortress." The Lord never enjoined those who begged relief from their pain to "offer it up." Nor does he do so to us, if we but seek, accept and work with his help.

Herein lies the key to praying the psalms fruitfully: to put ourselves in place of the psalmist, in place of the individual or the community for whom he speaks. As the psalms sing of the human condition, so do they sing of salvation history. The songs of Israel's liberation through the Lord's saving help are the songs of each individual's liberation through the cross of Christ. The "we" of the psalms must become the "I" of our prayer. I ought to be able to proclaim, *"My* help is in the name of the Lord" (Ps 124), and "When the Lord delivered *me* from bondage it was like a dream" (Ps 126). Then I will grasp my unique role in the economy of salvation.

Praying the Liturgy of the Hours

Getting into praying Morning or Evening Prayer is not as daunting as it may at first appear. A number of abridged, "user-friendly" versions are available (see p. 36) for those who wish to incorporate it into their prayer life. Dip into it; get the flavor of it. You need not feel obliged to pray all the Hours, or to pray them every day, or even to pray any one Hour in its entirety.

When you pray the Liturgy of the Hours you may find yourself praying a psalm whose mood does not correspond with your own mood at that time; perhaps you are faced with a joyful psalm of praise when you are feeling low, or perhaps a psalm of desperation turns up just when you are on top of the world. This should not matter. The Liturgy of the Hours is the prayer of the entire Church. When we pray it we pray for and with the entire Church community; we join our voices with the universal Church, whether it be the person next to us at Sunday Mass or with unknown people thousands of miles away.

The psalms are stirring songs and beautiful poetry, but, above all, they are an inexhaustible treasury of prayer material. Let none of us hesitate to make the psalms our prayer friends. Once we have made them and their language our own, we will have that much more to bring to our communal liturgies; we need never fear feeling that liturgical prayer is something "out there" that "they" are doing. And at the same time, we will find our enriched experience of liturgical prayer nourishing those times when we go to our inner room to pray to our Father in private.

Implementing the Liturgy of the Hours in the Parish

The question is often asked, "When can we celebrate the Liturgy of the Hours? Will people come out for such a celebration?" Sections of the Hours can be celebrated during the "privileged" times of the liturgical year, such as Advent/Christmas and Lent/Easter. People generally will take advantage of these additional opportunities to join in the Church's prayer.

A good way to begin implementing the celebration of the Hours in your parish would be to restore the tradition of Sunday Vespers or Sunday Evening Prayer during the seasons of the Church year. In many parishes these celebrations have become a tradition, part of the parish's celebration of Sunday. The celebration of Evening Prayer may also be celebrated on weekday evenings. Some parishes have set aside a time such as 5:30 for the daily celebration of Evening Prayer, while others have chosen a time like 7:45 for celebrating it. This affords people who will be coming to the church for meetings and other activities the opportunity to join in the prayer of the Church. In fact, some parishes have agreed to begin all parish activities with the celebration of Evening Prayer in the church. At the conclusion of the prayer, the various groups can then go off to their meetings and activities.

Morning Prayer can easily be worked into the morning schedule of the parish. I have found a good deal of success celebrating Morning Prayer at 8:30. Although there is a celebration of the Eucharist at 8:00 and at 9:00, people have remained, or have come early to celebrate this prayer of the Church. For others, this hour is convenient, and they come for Morning

Prayer and go off to work.

In the celebration of the Hours, the principle of "progressive solemnity" needs to be operative. This principle

> is one that recognizes several intermediate stages between singing the office in full and just reciting all the parts. Its application offers the possibility of a rich and pleasing variety. The criteria are the particular day or hour being celebrated, the character of the individual elements comprising the office, the size and composition of the community, as well as the number of singers available in the circumstances. (LOH, #273)

While a full complement of ministers (presider, assistant, cantor, musicians, reader) allows for the celebration of the Hours in the fullest sense, minimally, a presider (ordained or non-ordained), cantor, and reader would be necessary. Although the psalms and canticles may be recited, of their very nature they call out for singing. It is often better to sing one psalm well than merely to recite the entire office.

Two strains have been operative in the reform of the Liturgy of the Hours. One model, the *Cathedral or Parochial Office,* is the more ancient tradition. This office would have been celebrated with a full complement of ministers and ministries, fixed psalmody (morning psalms/evening psalms), and selective reading of the scriptures. As monastic ideals and spirituality became dominant, the *Cathedral Office* virtually disappeared, and was replaced by a *Monastic Office.* This office is characterized by continuous reading of the scriptures and the psalter, and by the disappearance of many of the ministries.

An Outline of Morning Prayer

> Opening Versicles
> Morning Hymn
> Psalmody
> > Morning psalm (and psalm prayer)
> > Additional psalmody
> > > (and/or Old Testament canticle)
>
> Scripture Reading
> Responsory
> > (or silent reflection)
>
> Gospel Canticle
> > (Zechariah's canticle: *Benedictus*)
>
> Intercessions
> Lord's Prayer
> Concluding Prayer
> Blessing and Dismissal
> > (Greeting of Peace)
> > (Final Hymn)

Morning Prayer begins with the invitation, "O God, come to my assistance" or "O Lord, open my lips," followed by the morning hymn. The hymn should reflect the character of morning and/or the particular season of the liturgical year. Following the hymn comes the psalmody.

Morning Prayer provides **two psalms and an Old Testament Canticle** throughout the four-week psalter.[1] This can, at times, prove to be unmanageable for some assemblies. The *Cathedral or Parochial Office* provides a fixed morning psalm and psalm of praise or doxology. As you begin to implement the celebration of the Hours in your parish, the fixed psalmody may work better. This fixed psalm would be analogous to the use of the common psalm for the season as opposed to the proper responsorial psalm at the Eucharist.

Following is a list of characteristic psalms of the Cathedral Office from which you can create a Morning Prayer service:
> Psalm 63
> Psalm 51 (Wednesdays and Fridays)
> *Additional Psalmody*
> > Psalms 8, 24, 42, 65, 66, 95, 96, 98, 99, 100, 108, 135

---

[1] See p. 17 for explanation.

Doxology
 148, 149, 150.

Regardless of which "model" of the office is used, after each psalm there is a pause for silent reflection. All then stand for the psalm prayer.[2]

At the conclusion of the psalmody, the reader proclaims the **scripture reading.**

> The reading of sacred Scripture, which, following an ancient tradition, takes place publicly in the liturgy, is to have special importance for all Christians, not only in the celebration of the eucharist, but also in the divine office. The reason that this reading is not the result of individual choice or devotion, but is the planned decision of the Church itself, is in order that in the course of the year the Bride of Christ may unfold the mystery of Christ "from his incarnation and birth until his ascension, the day of Pentecost, and the expectation of the blessed hope of the Lord's return." In addition, the reading of sacred Scripture in the liturgical celebration is always accompanied by prayer in order that the reading may have greater effect and that, in turn, prayer — especially the praying of the psalms — may gain fuller understanding and become more fervent and devout because of the reading. (LOH, #140)

The scripture reading is then followed by a brief **responsory.** This is "a kind of acclamation" which "enables the word of God to penetrate more deeply into the mind and heart of the person reciting or listening" (LOH, #172). The responsory should preferably be sung, or it may be replaced by a period of silent prayer.

The **Gospel Canticle,** the *Benedictus,* is then sung by the assembly. All stand and make the sign of the cross as the canticle is begun. The Gospel Canticle should be treated with the same dignity and solemnity as the proclamation of the Gospel at Mass.

The **intercessions** are said or sung following the Gospel Canticle. The presider invites prayer for various intentions, to which the assembly responds.

[2]See p. 12 for explanation.

The invocations or intercessions at Morning Prayer are slightly different in tone from the general intercessions at Mass. They serve to commend or consecrate the entire day to God. The intercessions conclude with the Lord's Prayer. The leader says a concluding prayer, and the celebration concludes with a blessing and dismissal.

Kinds of Psalmody

Liturgical Music Today (cf. #35-43) gives a brief but thorough explanation of the various methods for singing the psalms. Psalms may be sung:

- in a **responsorial** style, where the assembly sings a common refrain, while the cantor or psalmist sings the verses
- in the **antiphonal** style, in which the assembly is divided into two sections and the psalm text shared between them
- in a **through-composed** setting *(in directum),* in which the musical material is not ordinarily repeated
- to **formula tones** (e.g., Gregorian plainsong tones), which place a musical pattern over the verse of the psalm. While it involves repetition, these tones are easily learned by most assemblies.
- **Metrical psalms** are metric paraphrases of the psalm texts. This musical form profoundly affects and alters the praying of the psalms as ritual, and thus it should not generally be used during the psalmody of the Liturgy of the Hours.

See p. 31 for a list of Musical Resources.

An Outline of Evening Prayer

Opening Versicles
  (or Service of Light/Lucernarium)
Evening Hymn
  (Thanksgiving)
Psalmody
  Evening psalm (and psalm prayer)
  Additional psalmody
    (and/or New Testament canticle)
Scripture Reading
Responsory
  (or silent reflection/homily)

Gospel Canticle
   (Mary's canticle: *Magnificat)*
Intercessions
Lord's Prayer
Concluding Prayer
Blessing and Dismissal
   (Greeting of Peace)
   (Final Hymn)

Evening Prayer may begin with the **versicle**, "O God, come to my assistance" and an evening hymn, or it may begin with a Service of Light or **Lucernarium.** The Lucernarium comes from the ancient practice of beginning Evening Prayer with the lighting of lamps which would provide necessary light for the service. The Service of Light proclaims Jesus Christ as the light of our world, and offers thanks and praise for his presence and action in our lives. If Evening Prayer is begun with the Service of Light, the assisting minister or presiding minister carries the paschal candle into the dimly lit church and proclaims, "Jesus Christ is the Light of the World," to which the assembly responds, "A light no darkness can overcome." As the candle is placed in the stand, additional candles are lighted, or other lights can be turned on. Meanwhile the evening hymn is sung. The hymn should reflect the character of evening and/or the feast being celebrated. The most ancient evening hymn, *Phos Hilaron* (O Radiant Light), dates from the second or third century.

Following the hymn, there may be an **Evening Thanksgiving for the day.** This thanksgiving is in the style of the Preface at the Eucharist, and blesses God for the gift of the day that has ended, the evening that is now upon us, and for the presence of Jesus Christ in our world. A good example of an Evening Thanksgiving can be found in *Praise God in Song.* John Melloh has adapted a prayer from the *Apostolic Tradition:*

> We praise and thank you, O God,
> through your Son, Jesus Christ our Lord,
> through whom you have enlightened us by revealing
> the light that never fades. Joy to all creatures,
> honor, feasting and delight.
> Night is falling and day's allotted span draws to a close.
> We have enjoyed your gift of daylight;
> brighten now our evening hours. . . .

The Liturgy of the Hours provides **two psalms and a New Testament canticle** for use during the four-week cycle of Evening Prayer. The *Cathedral* or *Parochial Office* would use Psalm 141 ("My prayers rise like incense") as a fixed psalm — the traditional psalm for Evening Prayer. This psalm may be accompanied by an offering of incense. Additional psalmody may then follow. After each psalm, there is a pause for silent prayer, and then the assembly stands for the psalm prayer.

The Liturgy of the Hours provides a complete cycle of **readings** for the celebration of Evening Prayer. These are generally short readings, chosen "to express briefly and succinctly a biblical phrase, theme or exhortation" (LOH, #156). However, a longer scripture reading may be chosen, and is to be preferred, in celebrations in common with the people. Following the reading, there may be a period of silent reflection or the responsory. A homily or choral anthem may then follow.

The assembly then stands for the **Gospel Canticle,** the *Magnificat*. During the singing of the *Magnificat* the altar and assembly may be incensed. A metrical setting of this canticle to a familiar tune (such as "Old Hundredth") can allow the assembly to join in the singing with ease.

After the Gospel Canticle the **intercessions** are said or sung in the same manner as at Morning Prayer. The intercessions at Evening Prayer are modeled on the intercessions at the Eucharist, with prayers for the whole Church, secular authorities, the poor, the sick, the needs of the whole world, and the faithful departed. The intercessions conclude with the Lord's Prayer. The presider then says a closing prayer, and there is a blessing and dismissal. A greeting of peace and a final hymn may be added.

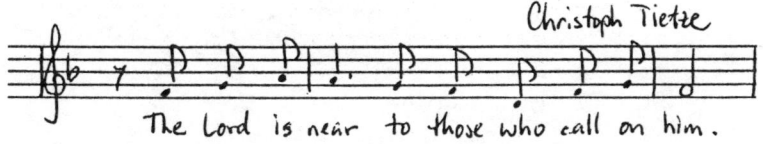

Musical Resources

Musical Resources for the Celebration of Morning Prayer

See list on p. 34 for publishers' names and addresses.

I. Introductory Versicles
    Worship, third edition   #3
    Gather   #15
    Praise God in Song   p. 22, 40, 56
    People's Mass Book   #750, 751

II. Morning Hymns
    Worship, third edition
        All Creatures of Our God and King   #520
        All People That on Earth Do Dwell   #669, 670
        Father, We Praise You   #4
        Joyful, Joyful We Adore You   #525
        Lord of All Hopefulness   #568
        Morning Has Broken   #674
        Morning of Splendor   #446
        On This Day, the First of Days   #662
        This Day God Gives Me   #673
        To God with Gladness Sing   #2
        When Morning Gilds the Skies   #675

    Gather
        A New Song   #214
        Blessed Be Our God   #236
        In Praise of His Name   #227
        Jubilate, Servite   #223

      God Is Alive   #2
      Praise His Name   #229
      Sing a New Song   #230
      You Are the Voice of the Living God #222

     People's Mass Book
      Sing Gently, O Earth   #752

     ICEL Resource Collection
      Lord God of Morning and of Night   #167
      Now that Daylight Fills the Sky   #168
      O Come, Let Us Sing to the Lord   #169

III. Psalmody
     The Gelineau Psalter
     Praise God in Song
     Worship, third edition
     Gather
     Glory and Praise

IV. Gospel Canticle
     psalm tone formula *(Christian Prayer)*
     metrical settings/through composed
       settings of Zechariah's Canticle
      Worship, third edition   #6
      Gather   #5
      People's Mass Book   #754
      ICEL Resource Collection   #349, 350

Musical Resources for the Celebration of Evening Prayer

See list on p. 34 for publishers' names and addresses.

  I. Introductory Versicles
     Worship, third edition   #10a
     Gather   #9
     Praise God in Song   p. 136, 158, 178
     People's Mass Book   #756

 II. Lucernarium/Evening Thanksgiving
     Worship, third edition   #13
     Gather   #9, 11
     Praise God in Song   p. 138, 160, 180
     People's Mass Book   #757

III. Evening Hymns
Worship, third edition
Christ, Mighty Savior #581
Day Is Done #677
Lord of All Hopefulness #568
O Gladsome Light #678
O Radiant Light #12
O Sun of Justice #424
The Day You Gave Us, Lord,
   Is Ended #678
Thy Strong Word Didst Cleave
   the Darkness #511
We Praise You Father #20

Gather
At Evening #320
Be Light for Our Eyes #244
Christ Is Alive #183
Eternal Lord of Love #160
God of Day and God of Darkness #319
Joyous Light of Heavenly Glory #318
O Radiant Light #10

ICEL Resource Collection
Abide with Me #171

IV. Psalmody
Evening Psalms
Psalm 141
Psalm 4, 23, 84, 91, 131, 136,
138, 145

V. Gospel Canticle: Magnificat
psalm tone formula *(Christian Prayer)*
Worship, third edition #15
Gather #14
Praise God in Song p. 152, 171, 194
People's Mass Book #762
ICEL Resource Collection #258

Resources and Publishers

1. *The Liturgy of the Hours: The General Instruction with Commentary* (A.-M. Roguet, OP; The Liturgical Press, Collegeville, MN) is an indispensable guide to the Liturgy of the Hours.

2. GIA Publications, 7404 S. Mason Avenue, Chicago, IL 60638.

   Worship, third edition
   Contains complete music and instructions for Morning Prayer and Evening Prayer, along with an extensive psalter.

   Worship, the Liturgy of the Hours. Leader's Guide
   Contains all the antiphons, psalm prayers, responsories, intercessions and collects for the four-week psalter for Morning Prayer and Evening Prayer for Sundays throughout the year, solemnities and feasts, and the Office of the Dead.

   Gather
   Contains a complete setting of Morning and Evening Prayer along with an extensive psalter.

   Praise God in Song
   Contains three musical settings of Morning Prayer and of Evening Prayer modeled on the Cathedral Office by Howard Hughes, David Clark Isele and Michael Joncas. Also contains additional psalmody, and extensive supplementary material and notes.

   The Grail-Gelineau Psalter
   Contains all 150 psalms and all the Old and New Testament canticles used in the celebration of the Hours, set to Gelineau psalmody.

   ICEL Resource Collection
   Contains hymnody and newly composed settings of the canticles for use in Morning and Evening Prayer.

   Praise God in Song: Night Prayer
   Contains the complete week of psalmody and prayer texts for Night Prayer.

   Hymnal for the Hours
   Contains a collection of hymns for Morning Prayer and Evening Prayer for use throughout the entire Church year.

Light and Peace
A complete setting of Morning Prayer and Evening Prayer by David Haas.

Psalm Praise
Published in England and distributed by GIA in the United States. Contains a good selection of psalmody in a variety of musical styles.

3. World Library Publications (WLP), 3759 Willow Road, Schiller Park, IL 60176

    People's Mass Book
    Contains a complete setting of Morning and Evening Prayer, along with an extensive psalter.

4. NALR, 10802 N. 23rd Avenue, Phoenix, AZ 85029

    Glory and Praise
    Contains extensive hymnody and psalmody in the contemporary idiom.

    Christian Daily Prayer
    Contains a complete setting of Morning Prayer, "As Morning Breaks" and Evening Prayer, "O Joyful Light" by Michael Joncas.

5. *Lutheran Book of Worship.* Augsburg/Fortress Publishing, 426 S. Fifth Street, Minneapolis, MN 55440
    Contains a complete pointed psalter, and setting of Morning, Evening and Night Prayer.

6. *The Hymnal 1982.* The Church Hymnal Corporation, 800 Second Avenue, New York, NY 10017
    The Hymnal of the Episcopal Church in America, which contains complete settings of Morning, Evening and Night Prayer.

7. *Morning Praise and Evensong.* Ave Maria Press, Notre Dame, IN
    Contains complete settings of Morning and Evening Prayer, together with psalm prayers, scripture readings, intercessions and collects.

8. FDLC, 401 Michigan Avenue, N.E., Box 29039, Washington, D.C. 20017

    Evening Prayer for Advent
    Evening Prayer for Lent
    Evening Prayer for Feasts of Mary

The Paschal Triduum
Obedient Unto Death
Musical settings of the Liturgy of the Hours for particular days and seasons, from the four-volume *Liturgy of the Hours*.

9. Catholic Book Publishing Company, New York, NY.

    The Liturgy of the Hours (4 volumes)
    Christian Prayer (1 volume)
    A Shorter Christian Prayer (1 volume)

Different editions of the Liturgy of the Hours — from complete to abridged — for those who wish to use this prayer in their daily life.

RVC Liturgical Series

These informative, yet brief and readable books have been written by a team of experienced liturgists for those actively involved in liturgical ministry as well as those seeking better to understand our Christian celebration.

Also available:

Our Liturgy: Your Guide to the Basics. Describes and discusses the nature of the many varieties of Liturgical Ministry, and presents clear explanations of Liturgical Objects and the Order of Mass. $4.25

The Great Seasons: Your Guide to Celebrating Advent-Christmas-Epiphany; Lent-Holy Week Triduum; The Easter Season. The Great Seasons celebrate in a special way the central aspects of the life and mystery of Christ, and *The Great Seasons* offers valuable insights to help with parish liturgy planning and to deepen personal liturgical celebration of these special times. $3.25

The Lector's Ministry: Your Guide to Proclaiming the Word. Not only provides basic practical advice on expressive reading and logistics which lectors and lector coordinators will find invaluable, but also encourages and inspires lectors to adopt a prophetic spirituality which will both nourish them personally and empower them to be eloquent witnesses of the word of God. $3.25

Contact publisher for information on bulk-order prices:
Resurrection Press
P.O. Box 248
Williston Park, NY 11596

Other Resurrection Press Publications

Of Life and Love. Fr. Jim Lisante. Foreword by John Powell. Preface by Archbishop Roger Mahony. $4.95

Award-winning columnist Fr. Jim Lisante offers his words of wisdom and encouragement in his first full-length book. Whatever your age, wherever you are in life, Fr. Jim's timely writings on Family Matters and Respect Life issues will challenge and inspire you.

"Excellent spiritual reading for parents, teens and teachers." *Praying*

I Shall Be Raised Up. A Scriptural Rosary for Lent. $1.95

This rosary meditation invites us to share with Jesus the anguish and desolation of his passion and to exult with him in the joy of his resurrection.

Verses from the Psalms preceding each Hail Mary serve as prayer guides. The Psalms are both prophecies about Jesus and prayers which he himself prayed, even in the hour of his greatest suffering. As we pray them with Jesus they lead us into the very depths of his soul.

I Shall Be Raised Up is an ideal private Lenten devotion, as well as particularly suitable for parish or prayer-group use. Musical texts and suggestions are provided.

Behold the Man. Seven Meditations on the Passion, Death and Resurrection of Jesus. Judy Marley, S.F.O. $2.95

These meditations lead us to imagine the mental suffering experienced by Jesus during his last days on earth. They take us on a journey from the poignant fellowship of the Last Supper to the ultimate absurdity — Golgotha — and beyond that to resurrection triumph.

Whether used in the privacy of your own prayer space or shared with the company of your prayer group, *Behold the Man* will be your passport to an unforgettable journey with Jesus.

READ THIS AMAZING STORY!
Give Them Shelter: The INN's Response to Hunger and Homelessness. Mike Moran. $5.95

Read about:
- the birth and growth of The INN's soup kitchens and emergency shelters
- the interfaith network of volunteers, food sources and donations which maintain The INN
- the breakdown of the racism, sexism and classism which are the underlying causes of hunger and homelessness.

INN Director Mike Moran shares with wisdom, humor and compassion the true story of fulfilling the scriptural mandate: GIVE THEM SHELTER.

Transformed by Love. The Way of Mary Magdalen. Sr. Margaret Magdalen, CSMV. Foreword by Jean Vanier. $5.95

Mary Magdalen is often associated with the woman who anointed Jesus at the home of Simon the Pharisee. Drawing from Mary's experience, Sister Margaret Magdalen shows the vital role of transformed passion as a God-given and essential part of the Christian life. Each chapter is based on an aspect of Mary's transformation through love, but widens out to embrace life experiences that touch us all — passion, penitence, fervor, darkness in prayer and freedom in relationships. It speaks to those who are broken in spirit, tangled in relationships and who feel that their situation is hopeless.

Our Spirit-Life Collection of Cassettes

Praying on Your Feet: A Contemporary Spirituality for Active Christians. Fr. Robert Lauder. 45 min. $5.95

Have you ever felt guilty about being too busy to pray? Fr. Lauder assures us that spirituality in today's world can be achieved on our feet as well as on our knees.

Annulment: Healing-Hope-New Life. Msgr. Thomas Molloy. 60 min. $5.95

In lay language Msgr. Molloy unravels the myth and mystery surrounding the annulment process. "A healing process, a time for meaningful reflection, growth and new beginnings."

Divided Loyalties: Church Renewal Through a Re-formed Priesthood. Anthony T. Padovano, Ph.D. S.T.D. 60 min. $6.95

In this thought-provoking and timely reflection on today's Church, Dr. Padovano exhorts us to fashion a new Church. His keen historical perspectives, powerful analogies and loving example of service will inspire you to make the Church a credible Church where hope, truth and mercy prevail.